Tokay Gecko

Tokay Gecko Pet Owner's Guide

Tokay Geckos Care, Behavior, Diet, Interaction, Costs and Health.

By

Ben Team

Published by: IMB Publishing

Table of Contents

About the Author

The author, Ben Team, is an environmental educator and author with over 16 years of professional reptile-keeping experience. Ben currently maintains www.FootstepsInTheForest.com, where he shares information, narration and observations of the natural world.

Foreword

Common pet reptile species primarily fall into one of two groups: Those that tolerate interaction and are physically appropriate for it, and those who do not meet these two criteria. Most casual reptile enthusiasts prefer those in the former group. They want to interact with their pet in a similar way that they would with a rodent, bird or hamster. These types of keepers normally prefer reptiles that are docile, personable and unlikely to bite, scratch or protest in other ways.

The appetite for these animals is so high that pet stores and swap meets are typically full of ball pythons, bearded dragons, leopard geckos and corn snakes. These animals are almost always tame and tolerate handling exceptionally well. However, other keepers approach the hobby with a different mindset. Somewhat like fish-keeping hobbyists, who almost never touch their animals or interact with them, these types of keepers are more interested in setting up enclosures and maintaining their animals with an emphasis on observation.

These keepers rarely gravitate toward bearded dragons and their ilk. These are the keepers that tend to find themselves drawn to chameleons, poison dart frogs or aquatic turtles. Additionally, many are interested in geckos – especially some of the most colorful.

Enter the tokay gecko (*Gekko gecko*). Though most notable for their typically defensive attitude and bold personalities, tokay geckos are beautiful lizards, who can be truly stunning in a well-planted habitat.

Tokay geckos have long been a mainstay of the imported reptile market, but they've remained relatively ignored thanks to their low price – it wasn't profitable to breed them, as the imported animals were incredibly inexpensive. However, as a few unreal-looking color mutations began popping up, the market started to change. Now that breeders were producing animals that sold for thousands of dollars, interest in the species exploded. But whether you are interested in obtaining some sort of mind-blowing mutant of a tokay gecko or one that looks just like the ones crawling through tropical forests, tokay geckos make excellent captives for keepers interested in observing their animal more than interacting with him.

PART I: THE TOKAY GECKO

Properly caring for any animal requires an understanding of the species and its place in the natural world. This includes digesting subjects as disparate as anatomy and ecology, diet and geography, and reproduction and physiology.

It is only by learning what your pet is, how it lives, what it does that you can achieve the primary goal of animal husbandry: Providing your pet with the highest quality of life possible.

Chapter 1: Tokay Gecko Description and Anatomy

Tokay geckos are beautiful and relatively large geckos. Although they share the same basic body plan as most other geckos, they are easy to identify on sight, once you become familiar with their physical characteristics.

Size

Tokay geckos hatch at about 3- to 4-inches (7 to 10 centimeters) in total length, and reach their full adult size over about 12 to 24 months' time. Upon reaching maturity, most tokay geckos are between 10 and 14 inches (25 to 35 centimeters) in total body length, of which roughly half is comprised of the tail.

Adults typically weigh between 5 and 8 ounces (150 to 225 grams), although occasional specimens exceeding 10 ounces (285 grams) have been reported.

Color and Pattern

Tokay geckos generally exhibit a light gray to powder blue ground color, which is covered in dozens of tiny orange to red spots. However, tokay geckos can change their colors quite a bit, and their ground color may range from nearly white to nearly black.

Males tend to be more brightly colored than females, but this isn't always a helpful criterion for distinguishing between the sexes.

The Tokay Gecko Head

Tokay geckos have relatively large, triangular heads and fairly indistinct necks. Large, bulging, gold-colored eyes sit on the sides of the head and feature a vertically elliptical pupil, which narrows to a slit in bright lighting and opens widely in the dark. The eyes feature no lids, so they cannot blink or close their eyes. Because the nose tapers sharply, these geckos can not only see to the sides, but they can see directly in front of their face as well.

Tokay geckos have relatively small ear openings, located behind their jawline. Their tympanums (ear drums) are visible if one looks inside the ear canal, but they are not as obvious as those of many other lizards. Despite the small size of their ears, tokay geckos have a good sense of hearing.

Tokay geckos have two nostrils, which are located near the front of the snout.

Mouth, Tongue and Teeth

Tokay geckos have large mouths that extend well past the eyes. Both the upper and lower gums are lined with tiny, sharp teeth, which are attached to the interior surface of the jawbone (called pleurodont dentition).

Most geckos are thought to be polyphodonts, who replace their teeth throughout their lives. By the time one tooth is ready to be lost, another is already developing to replace it.

Tokay geckos have thick, muscular tongues. In addition to playing a role in prey capture, geckos use their tongues to help groom themselves.

For example, to clean debris from their eyes – an important ability for an animal with no eyelids.

Limbs and Feet

Tokay geckos have four strong limbs, each of which extends laterally from the body. This arrangement allows the lizards to move effectively while climbing on tree trunks or scurrying across the ground below.

Geckos have very unique feet, which are highly specialized for their arboreal lifestyle. Like most other lizards, tokay geckos possess five toes on their feet. Their toes are covered in microscopic hairs, called setae, which allow the geckos to cling to smooth surfaces.

Vent

Tokay geckos have a small opening – called the vent – on their ventral surface, near the base of the tail. The vent leads directly to the cloaca, and serves as the final exit point for waste, urates and eggs. When lizards defecate, release urates or copulate, the vent opens slightly.

Tail

Tokay geckos have long tails that help them keep their balance and maneuver more effectively through the dense foliage of their natural habitat.

Like most other geckos, tokay geckos will jettison their tails to help escape from predators. Although they will usually regenerate their tails, the regrown tails rarely reach the same size as the original.

Internal Organs

The internal anatomy of tokay geckos differs relatively little from that of other lizards or tetrapods in general.

Geckos draw oxygen in through their nostrils; pipe it through the trachea and into the lungs. Here, blood exchanges carbon dioxide for oxygen, before it is pumped to the various body parts via the heart and blood vessels.

While the gecko's heart features only three true chambers (two atria and a single ventricle), a septum keeps the ventricle divided at most times, allowing the heart to operate similarly to a four-chambered, mammalian heart. This means that in practice, geckos keep their oxygenated and deoxygenated blood relatively separate in the heart.

Their digestive system is comprised of an esophagus, stomach, small intestine, large intestine and a terminal chamber called the cloaca. The stomach has some ability to stretch to accommodate food.

The liver resides near the center of the animal's torso, with the gall bladder sitting directly behind it. While the gall bladder stores bile, the liver provides a number of functions relating to digestion, metabolism and filtration. Kidneys, which lie almost directly behind the lungs, filter wastes from the lizard's bloodstream.

Geckos control their bodies via their brain and nervous system. Their endocrine and exocrine glands work much as they do in other vertebrates.

Reproductive Organs

Like all squamates, male tokay geckos have paired reproductive organs, called hemipenes. When not in use, males keep their hemipenes inside the bases of their tails. When they attempt to mate with a female, they evert one of the hemipenes and insert it into the female's cloaca.

These hemipenes create a slightly distinct bulge at the base of the geckos' tails. Some keepers learn to use this characteristic to distinguish males from females, but it is easier to note the presence or lack of waxy secretions emerging from the lizard's preanal pores. Males produce waxy secretions while females do not.

The paired nature of the male sex organs ensures that males can continue to breed if they suffer injury to one of the hemipenes. This paired arrangement also allows male geckos to mate with females on either side of their body.

Females have paired ovaries, which produce ova (eggs), and they have paired oviducts, which store the eggs after they are released from the ovaries.

The eggs are shelled and held inside the oviducts until it is time to deposit the eggs. At this time, the eggs are passed from the oviducts into the cloaca and out of the body via the vent.

Females also possess two calcium rich deposits in the throat. The calcium deposits are easily observed when the female opens her mouth.

Chapter 2: Tokay Gecko Biology and Behavior

Tokay geckos exhibit a number of biological and behavioral adaptations that allow them to survive in their natural habitats.

Shedding

Like other scaled reptiles, tokay geckos shed their old skin to reveal new, fresh skin underneath. Tokay geckos do not always shed their skin in one piece, as most snakes do, instead, they often allow the skin to break into a few, large pieces.

Tokay geckos often consume their shed skin, in order to recover any nutrients present in the old, dead cells.

Metabolism and Digestion

Tokay geckos are ectothermic ("cold-blooded") animals, whose internal metabolism depends on the gecko's body temperature. When geckos are warm, their bodily functions proceed more rapidly; when geckos are cold, their bodily functions proceed slowly.

This also means that tokay geckos digest more effectively at suitably warm temperatures than they do at suboptimal temperatures. Their appetites also vary with temperature, and if the temperatures drop below the preferred range, they may cease feeding entirely.

A gecko's body temperature largely follows ambient air temperatures, but they also absorb and reflect radiant heat, such as that coming from the sun. The lizards try to keep their body temperature within the preferred range by employing behaviors that allow them to adjust their temperature.

For example, geckos may bask to warm their temperature when they are too cool. This typically involves orienting their body so that they are perpendicular with the sun's rays. Some individuals may exhibit darker colors when basking to help absorb more infrared rays.

By contrast, when it is necessary to cool off, tokay geckos may move into the shade or gape their mouths to release excess heat.

However, in practice, tokay geckos rarely employ such strategies. Their native habitats provide them with suitable temperatures for most of their lives, so they just allow their body temperatures to fluctuate with the rising and falling temperatures.

Growth Rate and Lifespan
Most geckos, including tokay geckos, grow relatively quickly and lead rapid, relatively brief lives.

After completing their incubation period, tokay geckos hatch from their eggs. They grow quickly, and most wild specimens probably reach maturity in about 12 to 24 months.

Most wild-living tokay geckos probably die within their first year of life – much like most other small lizard species. However, those that reach adulthood probably live for four or five years. Nevertheless, captive individuals, who enjoy a predator- and parasite-free lifestyle may live for 10 years of more.

Foraging Behavior
Tokay geckos feed primarily on invertebrates, but large individuals will also consume small lizards, frogs, rodents or birds from time to time.

Insects are probably primarily captured opportunistically, such as when a roach or spider crawls onto the perch of one of these lizards. Once they see the potential prey item, the lizards focus both eyes on it and adjust their bodies, to move within the optimum range before pouncing.

Tokay geckos usually squeeze down on the prey item several times to incapacitate it, before swallowing. However, some prey may be swallowed alive.

Diel and Seasonal Activity
Wild-living tokay geckos are almost exclusively nocturnal, although they may be active at any time of day or night in captivity. They typically rise shortly after sunset and remain active for a few hours before settling back in to their hiding place.

Often, tokay geckos will sleep in places that provide some protection from predators, such as under the bark of a tree or on the underside of a leaf.

Mating usually takes place during the rainy season. Tokay geckos remain active throughout most of the year, although they typically refrain from breeding during the dry season.

Defensive Strategies and Tactics

Tokay geckos are cryptic animals that blend well with their environment. Additionally, tokay geckos possess unusual bumps and projections; these features disrupt their outlines, which further help to camouflage the lizards.

Tokay geckos may attempt to flee from predators that see through their camouflaged patterns, or they may face adversaries and gape their mouths or bite. As mentioned before, tokay geckos may shed their tails when threatened. Once disarticulated, the tail will wiggle and writhe for several minutes, hopefully keeping the attention of the predator, while the gecko can escape.

Their nocturnal lifestyle and secretive habits also provide inherent protective benefits to the lizards.

Reproduction

Females may retain the sperm from a single mating and deposit multiple clutches of eggs over the course of the breeding season. Males likely defend their established territory from other males.

Tokay geckos emit a loud vocalization as part of their territorial behavior. The sound, which varies widely, as often been described as sounding like "toe-kay," which eventually became the lizard's common name.

Chapter 3: Classification and Taxonomy

Geckos are a well-defined group of lizards, who all spring from a common ancestor, and tokay geckos are a well-defined species within this group. While their taxonomy has been subject to a few revisions, there is no doubt that these lizards represent a distinct species.

But before delving more deeply into the classification and taxonomy of tokay geckos, it is helpful to begin with a broader context.

Although the taxonomy of lizards is the subject of great debate, the Integrated Taxonomic Information System currently classifies all of the living geckos in the suborder Gekkota. Gekkota contains seven different families, including Gekkonidae, Carphodactylidae, Diplodactylidae, Eublepharidae, Phyllodactylidae, Pygopodidae and Sphaerodactylidae.

Tokay geckos are members of the family Gekkonidae, along with Madagascar's day geckos (*Phelsuma* spp.) and the leaf tail geckos (*Uroplatus* spp.).

Tokay geckos exhibit some variability within the species, and two subspecies are currently recognized by some authorities: *Gekko gecko gecko*, which lives throughout most of the species' range, and *Gekko gecko azhari*, which is restricted to the area around Bangladesh, Bhutan and Nepal.

Chapter 4: The Tokay Gecko's World

To maintain a tokay gecko successfully, you must understand the animal's native habitat and provide a reasonable facsimile of it.

Range

Tokay geckos are found throughout most of southeastern Asia, including portions of Myanmar, Thailand, Laos, Vietnam, Cambodia, Bangladesh, Bhutan, Nepal and parts of China.

They have also been introduced to several locations outside of this historical range, including Belize and the state of Florida in the southern United States. It is possible that they've been introduced to several other locations, but have gone unnoticed.

Climate

Southeast Asia has a warm, tropical climate. Although it remains somewhat damp all year long, there is a distinct rainy season, stretching from roughly October to February, although it varies slightly from one region to the next.

Habitat

Within their range, tokay geckos occur in a variety of different forest habitats, including those in the coastal lowlands, as well as those at higher elevations in the interior. They are also likely to be found in human-disturbed areas within these forests; tokay geckos even turn up in urban areas from time to time, and they are frequently seen perched near street lamps and other insect-attracting lights after dark.

Status in the Wild

Because tokay geckos are common in their native range and have been introduced to a number of other locations around the globe, they are unlikely to disappear in the near future.

Nevertheless, collection for the pet trade and habitat destruction both threaten the species, as they do most other reptiles common to the pet trade.

Natural Diet

Little research has been conducted on the feeding habits of wild-living tokay geckos, so the specific food items they prefer remain unknown.

Nevertheless, some of the primary invertebrate clades that tokay geckos prey upon include:

- Lepidopterans (adult butterflies, moths, skippers and larvae)
- Coleopterans (adult beetles and larvae)
- Dipterans (adult flies, crane flies, mosquitoes and larvae)
- Orthopterans (grasshoppers, katydids and crickets)
- Mollusks (snails and slugs)
- Annelids (earthworms)
- Arachnids (spiders and harvestmen)

Natural Predators

Virtually every large or medium-sized predator that shares habitat with tokay geckos represents a potential threat. Nevertheless, the primary predators of tokay geckos are probably large birds, snakes and small mammalian predators.

PART II: TOKAY GECKO HUSBANDRY

Once equipped with a basic understanding of what tokay geckos *are* (Chapter 1 and Chapter 3), where they *live* (Chapter 4), and what they *do* (Chapter 2) you can begin learning about their captive care.

Animal husbandry is an evolving pursuit. Keepers shift their strategies frequently as they incorporate new information and ideas into their husbandry paradigms.

There are few "right" or "wrong" answers, and what works in one situation may not work in another. Accordingly, you may find that different authorities present different, and sometimes conflicting, information regarding the care of these geckos.

In all cases, you must strive to learn as much as you can about your pet and its natural habitat, so that you may provide it with the best quality of life possible.

Chapter 5: Tokay Geckos as Pets

Tokay geckos can make rewarding pets, but you must know what to expect before adding one to your home and family. This includes not only understanding the nature of the care they require, but also the costs associated with this care.

Assuming that you feel confident in your ability to care for a gecko and endure the associated financial burdens, you can begin seeking your individual pet.

Understanding the Commitment

Keeping a tokay gecko as a pet requires a substantial commitment. You will be responsible for your pet's well-being for the rest of its life. Although tokay geckos are not particularly long-lived animals, their lifespans are not trivial.

Can you be sure that you will still want to care for your pet several years in the future? Do you know what your living situation will be? What changes will have occurred in your family? How will your working life have changed over this time?

You must consider all of these possibilities before acquiring a new pet. Failing to do so often leads to apathy, neglect and even resentment, which is not good for you or your pet lizard.

Neglecting your pet is wrong, and in some locations, a criminal offense. You must continue to provide quality care for your gecko, even once the novelty has worn off, and it is no longer fun to clean the cage and purchase crickets a few times a week.

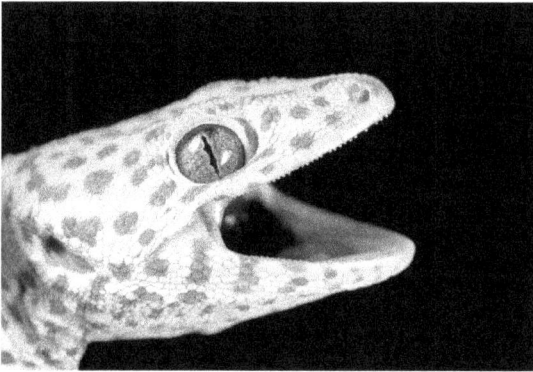

You can see the tokay gecko's small, sharp teeth above.

Once you purchase a gecko, its well-being becomes your responsibility until it passes away at the end of a long life, or you have found someone who will agree to adopt the animal for you. Unfortunately, this is rarely an easy task. You may begin with thoughts of selling your pet to help recoup a small part of your investment, but these efforts will largely fall flat.

While professional breeders may profit from the sale of tokay geckos, amateurs are at a decided disadvantage. Only a tiny sliver of the general population is interested in reptilian pets, and only a small subset of these are interested in keeping tokay geckos.

Of those who are interested in acquiring a tokay gecko, most would rather start fresh, by *purchasing* a small hatchling or juvenile from an established breeder, rather than adopting your questionable animal *for free.*

After having difficulty finding a willing party to purchase or adopt your animal, many owners try to donate their pet to a local zoo. Unfortunately, this rarely works either.

Zoos are not interested in your pet gecko, no matter how pretty he is and how readily he snatches crickets from your fingers. He is a pet with little to no reliable provenance and questionable health status. This is simply not the type of animal zoos are eager to add to their multi-million dollar collections.

Zoos obtain most of their animals from other zoos and museums; failing that, they obtain their animals directly from their land of origin. As a rule, they do not accept donated pets.

No matter how difficult it becomes to find a new home for your unwanted gecko, you must never release non-native reptiles into the wild. Geckos can colonize places outside their native range, with disastrous results for the ecosystem's native fauna.

Additionally, released or escaped reptiles cause a great deal of distress to those who are frightened by them. This leads local municipalities to adopt pet restrictions or ban reptile keeping entirely.

While the chances of an escaped or released gecko harming anyone are very low, it is unlikely that those who fear reptiles will see the threat as minor.

The Costs of Captivity

Reptiles are often marketed as low-cost pets. While true in a relative sense (the costs associated with dog, cat, horse or tropical fish husbandry are often much higher than they are for tokay geckos), potential keepers must still prepare for the financial implications of tokay gecko ownership.

At the outset, you must budget for the acquisition of your pet, as well as the costs of purchasing or constructing a habitat. Unfortunately, while many keepers plan for these costs, they typically fail to consider the on-going costs, which will quickly eclipse the initial startup costs.

Startup Costs

One surprising fact most new keepers learn is the enclosure and equipment will often cost more than the animal does (except in the case of very high-priced specimens).

Prices fluctuate from one market to the next, but in general, the least you will spend on a healthy tokay gecko is about $25 (£20), while the least you will spend on the *initial* habitat and assorted equipment will be about $50 (£40). Replacement equipment and food will represent additional (and ongoing) expenses.

Examine the charts on the following pages to get an idea of three different pricing scenarios. While the specific prices listed will vary based on innumerable factors, the charts are instructive for first-time buyers.

The first scenario details a budget-minded keeper, trying to spend as little as possible. The second example estimates the costs for a keeper with a moderate budget, and the third example provides a case study for extravagant shoppers, who want an expensive gecko and top-notch equipment.

These charts are only provided estimates; your experience may vary based on a variety of factors.

Inexpensive Option

Wild Caught Tokay Gecko	$10 (£8)
Economy Homemade Habitat	$25 (£20)
Heat Lamp Fixture and Bulbs	$20 (£16)
Plants, Substrate, Hides, etc.	$20 (£16)
Infrared Thermometer	$35 (£24)
Digital Indoor-Outdoor Thermometer	$20 (£16)
Water Dish, Forceps, Spray Bottles, Misc.	$20 (£16)
Total	**$150 (£116)**

Moderate Option

Captive Bred Tokay Gecko Hatchling	$25 (£20)
Premium Homemade Habitat	$100 (£80)
Heat Lamp Fixture and Bulbs	$20 (£16)
Plants, Substrate, Hides, etc.	$20 (£16)
Infrared Thermometer	$35 (£24)
Digital Indoor-Outdoor Thermometer	$20 (£16)
Water Dish, Forceps, Spray Bottles, Misc.	$20 (£16)
Total	**$240 (£188)**

Premium Option

Caramel Albino Tokay Gecko	$1500 (£1200)
Premium Commercial Cage	$100 (£160)
Heat Lamp Fixture and Bulbs	$20 (£16)
Plants, Substrate, Hides, etc.	$20 (£16)
Infrared Thermometer	$35 (£24)
Digital Indoor-Outdoor Thermometer	$20 (£16)
Water Dish, Forceps, Spray Bottles, Misc.	$20 (£16)
Total	**$1715 (£1442)**

Ongoing Costs

The ongoing costs of tokay gecko ownership primarily fall into one of three categories: food, maintenance and veterinary care.

Food costs are the most significant of the three, but they are relatively consistent and somewhat predictable. Some maintenance costs are easy to calculate, but things like equipment malfunctions are impossible to predict with any certainty. Veterinary expenses are hard to predict and vary wildly from one year to the next.

Food Costs

Food is the single greatest ongoing cost you will experience while caring for your tokay gecko. To obtain a reasonable estimate of your yearly food costs, you must consider the number of meals you will feed your pet per year and the cost of each meal.

The amount of food your gecko will consume will vary based on numerous factors, including his size, the average temperatures in his habitat and his health.

As a ballpark number, you should figure that you'll need about $5 (£4) per week – roughly $250 (£205) per year -- for food. You could certainly spend more or less than this, but that is a reasonable estimate for back-of-the-envelope calculations.

Veterinary Costs

While you should always seek veterinary advice at the first sign of illness, it is probably not wise to haul your healthy tokay gecko to the vet's office for no reason – they don't require "checkups" or annual vaccinations as some other pets may. Accordingly, you shouldn't incur any veterinary expenses unless your pet falls ill.

However, veterinary care can become very expensive, very quickly. In addition to a basic exam or phone consultation, your lizard may need cultures, x-rays or other diagnostic tests performed. In light of this, wise keepers budget at least $200 to $300 (£160 to £245) each year to cover any emergency veterinary costs.

Maintenance Costs

It is important to plan for both routine and unexpected maintenance costs. Commonly used items, such as paper towels, disinfectant and top soil are rather easy to calculate. However, it is not easy to know how many burned out light bulbs, cracked misting units or faulty thermostats you will have to replace in a given year.

Those who keep their tokay geckos in simple enclosures will find that about $50 (£40) covers their yearly maintenance costs. By contrast, those who maintain elaborate habitats may spend $200 (£160) or more each year.

Always try to purchase frequently used supplies, such as light bulbs, paper towels and disinfectants in bulk to maximize your savings. It is often beneficial to consult with local reptile-keeping clubs, who often pool their resources to attain greater buying power.

Myths and Misunderstandings

Myth: Lizards that shed their tails will readily produce a replacement tail.

Fact: Most lizards that autotomize their tails do grow a replacement tail. However, some geckos – including tokay geckos – fail to always regenerate their tails very well. Some will grow back looking relatively similar to the original, but many other regenerated tails are dark and lack the shape and pliability of the original.

Myth: Tokay geckos need "friends" or they will get lonely.

Fact: Although they can be kept in small groups, consisting of two or three females and a single male, tokay geckos are essentially solitary animals in the wild, who spend the bulk of their lives alone. Accordingly, they will never "miss" having cagemates, and you should not feel obligated to keep them in a communal setting.

Myth: Reptiles grow in proportion to the size of their cage and then stop.

Fact: Reptiles do no such thing. Most healthy lizards, snakes and turtles grow throughout their lives, although the rate of growth slows with age (a very few stop growing with maturity, although this is not influenced by the size of their cage).

Placing them in a small cage in an attempt to stunt their growth is an unthinkably cruel practice, which is more likely to sicken or kill your pet than stunt its growth.

Providing a tokay gecko with an inadequately spacious cage is a sure recipe for illness, maladaptation and eventual death. And because tokay geckos are not gigantic animals anyway, it just doesn't make sense to try to stunt their growth with a small cage – even if the practice worked.

Myth: Geckos must eat live food.

Fact: Most geckos – in fact, most insectivorous lizards – require live insects for food. However, some owners manage to tempt their tokays into eating dead insects or mice. This usually requires "animating" the food item by moving it around with a pair of tongs.

Myth: Reptiles have no emotions and do not suffer.

Fact: While geckos have very primitive brains and do not have emotions comparable to those of higher mammals, they can absolutely suffer. Always treat reptiles with the same compassion you would offer a dog, cat or horse.

Myth: Tokay geckos are vicious lizards that bite at every chance.

Fact: While tokay geckos are pretty defensive lizards, some do calm down and accept brief interactions with their keeper. This is most common among captive bred offspring; wild caught adults rarely tolerate being touched by their keeper.

Acquiring Your Tokay Gecko

Modern reptile enthusiasts can acquire tokay geckos from a variety of sources, each with a different set of pros and cons.

Pet stores are one of the first places many people see tokay geckos, and they become the de facto source of pets for many beginning keepers. While they do offer some unique benefits to prospective keepers, pet stores are not always the best place to purchase a gecko; so, consider all of the available options, including breeders and reptile swap meets, before making a purchase.

Pet Stores

Pet stores offer a number of benefits to keepers shopping for tokay geckos, including convenience: They usually stock all of the equipment your new lizard needs, including cages, heating devices and food items.

Additionally, they offer you the chance to inspect the lizard up close before purchase. In some cases, you may be able to choose from more than one specimen. Many pet stores provide health guarantees for a short period, that provides some recourse if your new pet turns out to be ill.

However, pet stores are not always the ideal place to purchase your new pet. Pet stores are retail establishments, and as such, you will usually pay more for your new pet than you would from a breeder.

Additionally, pet stores rarely know the pedigree of the animals they sell, and they will rarely know the lizard's date of birth, or other pertinent information.

Other drawbacks associated with pet stores primarily relate to the staff's inexperience. While some pet stores concentrate on reptiles and may educate their staff about proper gecko care, many others provide incorrect advice to their customers.

It is also worth considering the increased exposure to pathogens that pet store animals endure, given the constant flow of animals through such facilities.

Reptile Expos
Reptile expos offer another option for purchasing a tokay gecko. Reptile expos often feature resellers, breeders and retailers in the same room, all selling various types of geckos and other reptiles.

Often, the prices at such events are quite reasonable and you are often able to select from many different lizards. However, if you have a problem, it may be difficult to find the seller after the event is over.

Breeders
Because they usually offer unparalleled information and support to their customers, breeders are generally the best place for most novices to shop for tokay geckos. Additionally, breeders often know the species well, and are better able to help you learn the husbandry techniques necessary for success.

For those seeking a particular type of tokay gecko, breeders are often the only option. You won't find many albino tokay geckos in pet stores, for example.

The primary disadvantage of buying from a breeder is that you must often make such purchases from a distance, either by phone or via the internet. Nevertheless, most established breeders are happy to provide you with photographs of the animal you will be purchasing, as well as his or her parents.

Selecting Your Gecko

Not all tokay geckos are created equally, so it is important to select a healthy individual that will give you the best chance of success.

Practically speaking, the most important criterion to consider is the health of the animal. However, the sex, age and history of the lizard are also important things to consider.

Health Checklist

Always check your gecko thoroughly for signs of injury or illness before purchasing it. If you are purchasing the animal from someone in a different part of the country, you must inspect it immediately upon delivery. Notify the seller promptly if the animal exhibits any health problems.

Avoid the temptation to acquire or accept a sick or injured animal in hopes of nursing him back to health. Not only are you likely to incur substantial veterinary costs while treating your new pet, you will likely fail in your attempts to restore the lizard to full health. Sick geckos rarely recover in the hands of novices.

Additionally, by purchasing injured or diseased animals, you incentivize poor husbandry on the part of the retailer. If retailers lose money on sick or injured animals, they will take steps to avoid this eventuality, by acquiring healthier stock in the first place, and providing better care for their charges.

As much as is possible, try to observe the following features:

- **Observe the lizard's skin**. It should be free of lacerations and other damage. Pay special attention to those areas that frequently sustain damage, such as the tip of the lizard's tail, the toes and the tip of the snout. A small cut or abrasion may be relatively easy to treat, but significant abrasions and cuts are likely to become infected and require significant treatment.

- Gently check the lizard's crevices and creases for mites and ticks. Mites are about the size of a flake of pepper, and they may be black, brown or red. Mites often move about on the lizard, whereas ticks – if attached and feeding – do not move. Avoid purchasing any animal that has either parasite. Additionally, you should avoid purchasing any other animals from this source, as they are likely to harbor parasites as well.

- Examine the lizard's eyes, ears and nostrils. The eyes should not be sunken, and they should be free of discharge. The nostrils should be clear and dry – lizards with runny noses or those who blow bubbles are likely to be suffering from a respiratory infection. However, be aware that lizards often get some water in their nostrils while drinking water. This is no cause for concern.

- Gently palpate the animal and ensure no lumps or anomalies are apparent. Lumps in the muscles or abdominal cavity may indicate parasites, abscesses or tumors.

- Observe the lizard's demeanor. Healthy lizards are aware of their environment and react to stimuli. When active, the lizard should calmly explore his environment. While you may wish to avoid purchasing an aggressive, defensive or flighty animal, these behaviors do not necessarily indicate a health problem.

- Check the lizard's vent. The vent should be clean and free of smeared feces. Smeared feces can indicate parasites or bacterial infections.
- Check the lizard's appetite. If possible, ask the retailer to feed the lizard a cricket, superworm or roach. A healthy gecko should usually exhibit a strong food drive, although failing to eat is not *necessarily* a bad sign – the lizard may not be hungry.

The Age
Hatchling tokay geckos are very fragile until they reach about one month of age. Before this, they are unlikely to thrive in the hands of beginning keepers.

Accordingly, most beginners should purchase two- or three-month-old juveniles, who have already become well established. Animals of this age tolerate the changes associated with a new home better than very young specimens do. Further, given their greater size, they will better tolerate temperature and humidity extremes than smaller animals will.

The Sex

Unless you are attempting to breed tokay geckos, you should select a male pet, as females are more likely to suffer from reproduction-related health problems than males are.

Most females will produce and deposit egg clutches upon reaching maturity, whether they are housed with a male or not. While this is not necessarily problematic, novices can easily avoid this unnecessary complication by selecting males as pets.

Quarantine

Because new animals may have illnesses or parasites that could infect the rest of your collection, it is wise to quarantine all new acquisitions. This means that you should keep any new animal as separated from the rest of your pets as possible. Only once you have ensured that the new animal is healthy should you introduce it to the rest of your collection.

During the quarantine period, you should keep the new lizard in a simplified habitat, with a paper substrate, water bowl, basking spot and a few hiding places. Keep the temperature and humidity at ideal levels.

It is wise to obtain fecal samples from your lizard during the quarantine period. You can take these samples to your veterinarian, who can check them for signs of internal parasites. Always treat any existing parasite infestations before removing the animal from quarantine.

Always tend to quarantined animals last, as this reduces the chances of transmitting pathogens to your healthy animals. Do not wash quarantined water bowls or cage furniture with those belonging to your healthy animals. Whenever possible, use completely separate tools for quarantined animals and those that have been in your collection for some time.

Always be sure to wash your hands thoroughly after handling quarantined animals, their cages or their tools. Particularly careful keepers wear a smock or alternative clothing when handling quarantined animals.

Quarantine new acquisitions for a minimum of 30 days; 60 or 90 days is even better. Many zoos and professional breeders maintain 180- or 360-day-long quarantine periods.

Chapter 6: Providing the Captive Habitat

In most respects, providing geckos with a suitable captive habitat entails functionally replicating the various aspects of their wild habitats.

In addition to providing your pet with an enclosure, you must provide the animal with the correct thermal environment, appropriate humidity, substrate, and suitable cage furniture.

Enclosure

Providing your tokay gecko with appropriate housing is and essential aspect of captive care. In essence, the habitat you provide to your pet becomes his world.

In "the old days," those inclined to keep reptiles had few choices with regard to caging. The two primary options were to build a custom cage from scratch or construct a lid to use with a fish aquarium.

By contrast, modern hobbyists have a variety of options from which to choose. In addition to building custom cages or adapting aquaria, dozens of different cage styles are available – each with different pros and cons.

Remember: There are few absolutes regarding reptile husbandry, and what works for most keepers and lizards may not work for you and your pet. Additionally, advanced keepers are often able to sidestep problems that trouble beginners.

Dimensions

Tokay geckos require only a modest amount of space to thrive. Ideally, each adult should have an enclosure with at least 2 to 4 square feet (180 to 360 square centimeters) of floor space, although some keepers provide less than this. Hatchlings and juveniles obviously require less space than adults do.

Tokay geckos appreciate a significant amount of vertical space in their cage. Try to provide your lizard with a habitat that is at least 2 feet (60 centimeters) tall.

Aquariums

Aquariums are popular choices for many pet reptiles and they are available at virtually every pet store in the country. However, they have a number of flaws that make them poor choices.

Aquariums are heavy, fragile and built in proportions that favor the behaviors of fish, rather than reptiles. The glass walls of an aquarium are difficult to clean, and can make your lizard feel like he is exposed.

Additionally, aquariums are only accessible through the top of the enclosure, which is problematic for a number of reasons. You'll have to move the cage lights before removing the top, and because tokay geckos often travel up when frightened, a top-opening cage can allow them to escape.

Commercial Cages

Commercially produced reptile enclosures are one of the best options for tokay gecko maintenance. They feature front-opening doors and they are usually made from lightweight, yet rugged plastic.

Many commercial cages feature internal light fixtures, but these serve as a double-edged sword: On the one hand, they may provide a convenient way to provide light or heat to the enclosure, but these lights can serve as a safety hazard for your pets. Additionally, the cracks and crevices surrounding the fixtures can provide your lizard with inaccessible hiding places.

Commercial cages are generally the most expensive option for tokay geckos, but their benefits strongly outweigh this additional expense.

Plastic Storage Containers

Plastic storage containers, such as those used for shoes, sweaters or food, are popular enclosure options for many reptiles, and large models work well for tokay gecko maintenance.

You'll need to make modifications to most plastic storage boxes to make them suitable for lizard maintenance, but they rarely present significant challenges.

For example, you'll need to add a series of small holes or cut out a "window" over which you can attach fine mesh screen.

Additionally, you may want to use the box in an orientation other than what the manufacturer intended. In other words, you may want to use the box in a vertical orientation, rather than a horizontal one, so you can provide greater height for your lizard's needs. Doing so may require you to build "feet" for the cage or some type of support pedestal.

Chapter 7: Establishing the Thermal Environment

Providing the proper thermal environment is one of the most important aspects of reptile husbandry. As ectothermic ("cold blooded") animals, tokay geckos rely on the surrounding temperatures to regulate the rate at which their metabolism operates.

Providing a proper thermal environment can mean the difference between a healthy, thriving gecko and one who spends a great deal of time at the veterinarian's office, battling infections and illness.

While individuals may demonstrate slightly different preferences, active tokay geckos generally prefer ambient temperatures in the low 80s Fahrenheit (about 26 to 30 degrees Celsius). Inactive (sleeping) tokay geckos prefer temperatures in the low 70s Fahrenheit (21 to 23 degrees Celsius).

While these are appropriate air temperatures for tokay geckos, they will also require a basking spot during the day, with a temperature of about 95 degrees Fahrenheit (35 degrees Celsius).

Providing your gecko with a suitable thermal environment requires the correct approach, the correct heating equipment and the tools necessary for monitoring the thermal environment.

Size-Related Heating Concerns

Before examining the best way to establish a proper thermal environment, it is important to understand that your lizard's body size influences the way in which he heats up and cools off.

Because volume increases more quickly than surface area does with increasing body size, small individuals experience more rapid temperature fluctuations than larger individuals do.

Accordingly, it is imperative to protect small individuals from temperature extremes. Conversely, larger tokay geckos are more tolerant of temperature extremes than smaller individuals are (though they should still be protected from temperature extremes).

Thermal Gradients

In the wild, tokay geckos move between different microhabitats so that they can maintain ideal body temperature as much as possible. You want to provide similar opportunities for your captive lizard by creating a thermal gradient.

The best way to do this is by clustering the heating devices at one end of the habitat, thereby creating a basking spot (the warmest spot in the enclosure).

The temperatures will slowly drop with increasing distance from the basking spot, which creates a *gradient* of temperatures. Barriers, such as branches and vegetation, also help to create shaded patches, which provide additional thermal options.

This mimics the way temperatures vary from one small place to the next in your pet's natural habitat. For example, a wild gecko may move under a piece of bark to escape the sun, or move onto an exposed branch to warm up on a cool morning.

By establishing a gradient in the enclosure, your captive gecko will be able to access a range of different temperatures, which will allow him to manage his body temperature just as his wild counterparts do.

Adjust the heating device until the surface temperatures at the basking spot are about 95 degrees Fahrenheit (35 degrees Celsius). Provide a slightly cooler basking spot for immature individuals, with maximum temperatures of about 90 degrees Fahrenheit (32 degrees Celsius).

Because there is no heat source at the other end of the cage, the ambient temperature will gradually fall as your lizard moves away from the heat source. Ideally, the cool end of the cage should be in the low 70s Fahrenheit (22 degrees Celsius).

The need to establish a thermal gradient is one of the most compelling reasons to use a roomy cage. In general, the larger the cage, the easier it is to establish a suitable thermal gradient.

Heating Equipment

There are a variety of different heating devices you can use to keep your tokay gecko's habitat within the appropriate temperature range.

Be sure to consider your choice carefully, and select the best type of heating device for you and your lizard.

Heat Lamps

Heat lamps are usually the best choice for supplying heat to your tokay gecko. Heat lamps consist of a reflector dome and an incandescent bulb. The light bulb produces heat (in addition to light) and the metal reflector dome directs the heat to a spot inside the cage.

You will need to clamp the lamp to a stable anchor or part of the cage's frame. Always be sure that the lamp is securely attached and will not be dislodged by vibration, children or pets.

Because fire safety is always a concern, and many keepers use high-wattage lightbulbs, opt for heavy-duty reflector domes with ceramic bases, rather than economy units with plastic bases. The price difference is negligible, given the stakes.

One of the greatest benefits of using heat lamps to maintain the temperature of your pet's habitat is the flexibility they offer. While you can adjust the amount of heat provided by heat tapes and other devices with a rheostat or thermostat, you can adjust the enclosure temperature provided by heat lamps in two ways:

- Changing the Bulb Wattage

The simplest way to adjust the temperature of your gecko's cage is by changing the wattage of the bulb you are using.

For example, if a 40-watt light bulb is not raising the temperature of the basking spot high enough, you may try a 60-watt bulb. Alternatively, if a 100-watt light bulb is elevating the cage temperatures higher than are appropriate, switching to a 60-watt bulb may help.

- Adjusting the Distance between the Heat Lamp and the Basking Spot

The closer the heat lamp is to the cage, the warmer the cage will be. If the habitat is too warm, you can move the light farther from the enclosure, which should lower the basking spot temperatures slightly.

However, the farther away you move the lamp, the larger the basking spot becomes. It is important to be careful that you do not move it to far away, which will reduce the effectiveness of the thermal gradient by heating the enclosure too uniformly. In very large cages, this may not compromise the thermal gradient very much, but in a small cage, it may eliminate the "cool side" of the habitat.

In other words, if your heat lamp creates a basking spot that is roughly 1-foot in diameter when it is 1inch away from the screen, it will produce a slightly cooler, but larger basking spot when moved back another 6 inches or so.

Ceramic Heat Emitters
Ceramic heat emitters are small inserts that function similarly to light bulbs, except that they do not produce any visible light – they only produce heat.

Ceramic heat emitters are used in reflector-dome fixtures, just as heat lamps are. The benefits of such devices are numerous:

- They typically last much longer than light bulbs do

- They are suitable for use with thermostats

- They allow for the creation of overhead basking spots, as lights do

- They can be used day or night

However, the devices do have three primary drawbacks:

- They are very hot when in operation

- They are much more expensive than light bulbs

- You cannot tell by looking if they are hot or cool. This can be a safety hazard – touching a ceramic heat emitter while it is hot is likely to cause serious burns.

Radiant Heat Panels
Quality radiant heat panels are a great choice for heating most reptile habitats, including those containing tokay geckos. Radiant heat panels are essentially heat pads that stick to the roof of the habitat.

They usually feature rugged, plastic or metal casings and internal reflectors to direct the infrared heat back into the cage.

Radiant heat panels have a number of benefits over traditional heat lamps and under tank heat pads:

- They do not produce visible light, which means they are useful for both diurnal and nocturnal heat production. They can be used in conjunction with fluorescent light fixtures during the day, and remain on at night once the lights go off.

- They are inherently flexible. Unlike many devices that do not work well with pulse-proportional thermostats, most radiant heat panels work well with on-off and pulse-proportional thermostats.

The only real drawback to radiant heat panels is their cost: radiant heat panels often cost about two to three times the price of light- or heat pad-oriented systems. However, many radiant heat panels outlast light bulbs and heat pads, a fact that offsets their high initial cost over the long term.

Heat Pads
Heat pads are an attractive option for many new keepers, but they are not without drawbacks.

- Heat pads have a high risk for causing contact burns.

- If they malfunction, they can damage the cage as well as the surface on which they are placed.

- They are more likely to cause a fire than heat lamps or radiant heat panels are.

However, if installed properly (which includes allowing fresh air to flow over the exposed side of the heat pad) and used in conjunction with a thermostat, they can be reasonably safe. With heat pads, it behooves the keeper to purchase premium products, despite the small increase in price.

Heat Tape
Heat tape is somewhat akin to a "stripped down" heat pad. In fact, most heat pads are simply pieces of heat tape that have already been connected and sealed inside a plastic envelope.

Heat tape is primarily used to heat large numbers of cages simultaneously. It is generally inappropriate for novices, and requires the keeper to make electrical connections. Additionally, a thermostat is always required when using heat tape.

Historically, heat tape was used to keep water pipes from freezing – not to heat reptile cages. While some commercial heat tapes have been designed specifically for reptiles, many have not. Accordingly, it may be illegal, not to mention dangerous, to use heat tapes for purposes other than for which they are designed.

Heat Cables
Heat cables are similar to heat tape, in that they heat a long strip of the cage, but they are much more flexible and easy to use. Many heat cables are suitable to use inside the cage, while others are designed for use outside the habitat.

Always be sure to purchase heat cables that are designed to be used in reptile cages. Those sold at hardware stores are not appropriate for use in a cage.

Heat cables must be used in conjunction with a thermostat, or, at the very least, a rheostat.

Hot Rocks
In the early days of commercial reptile products, faux rocks, branches and caves with internal heating elements were very popular. However, they have generally fallen out of favor among modern keepers. These rocks and branches were often made with poor craftsmanship and cheap materials, causing them to fail and produce tragic results. Additionally, many keepers used the rocks improperly, leading to injuries, illnesses and death for many unfortunate reptiles.

Heated rocks are not designed to heat an entire cage; they are designed to provide a localized source of heat for the reptile. Nevertheless, many keepers tried to use them as the primary heat source for the cage, resulting in dangerously cool cage temperatures.

When lizards must rely on small, localized heat sources placed in otherwise chilly cages, they often hug these heat sources for extended periods of time. This can lead to serious thermal burns –

whether or not the unit functions properly. This illustrates the key reason why these devices make adequate supplemental heat sources, but they should not be used as primary heating sources.

Modern heated rocks utilize better features, materials and craftsmanship than the old models did, but they still offer few benefits to the keeper or the kept. Additionally, any heating devices that are designed to be used inside the cage necessitate passing an electric cable through a hole, which is not always easy to accomplish. However, some cages do feature passageways for chords.

Nocturnal Temperatures
Because tokay geckos safely tolerate temperatures in the low-70s Fahrenheit (21 to 22 degrees Celsius) at night, most keepers can allow their tokay gecko's habitat to fall to ambient room temperature at night.

Because it is important to avoid using lights on your gecko's habitat at night, those living in homes with lower nighttime temperatures will need to employ additional heat sources. Most such keepers accomplish this through the use of ceramic heat emitters.

Thermometers
It is important to monitor the cage temperatures very carefully to ensure your pet stays health. Just as a water test kit is an aquarist's best friend, quality thermometers are some of the most important husbandry tools for reptile keepers.

Ambient and Surface Temperatures
Two different types of temperature are relevant for pet lizards: ambient temperatures and surface temperatures.

The ambient temperature in your animal's enclosure is the air temperature; the surface temperatures are the temperatures of the objects in the cage. Both are important to monitor, as they can differ widely.

Measure the cage's ambient temperatures with a digital thermometer. An indoor-outdoor model will feature a probe that allows you to measure the temperature at both ends of the thermal gradient at once. For example, you may position the thermometer at the cool side of the cage, but attach the remote probe to a branch near the basking spot.

Because standard digital thermometers do not measure surface temperatures well, use a non-contact, infrared thermometer for such measurements. These devices will allow you to measure surface temperatures accurately from a short distance away.

Chapter 8: Lighting the Enclosure

Lighting is a contentious and controversial subject among lizard keepers. The topic most commonly comes up among keepers of diurnal lizard species, such as bearded dragons (*Pogona vitticeps*), monitor lizards (*Varanus* spp.) and various iguanas (*Iguana* spp.), but even gecko keepers debate the subject from time to time.

Diurnal lizards often have very specific light requirements, which the sun meets (and greatly exceeds) with ease, yet are difficult to replicate with light bulbs. Accordingly, there is a great deal such keepers must understand about light to make sure they meet their pet's needs.

However, most nocturnal species are assumed to prefer dim cages, and as a rule, they are not thought to have the same lighting requirements that most diurnal lizards do.

Most tokay gecko keepers elect not to provide any lighting for their pets, while others feel that sun-mimicking lights are helpful for their lizards and include them in their pet's habitat. You'll just have to learn as much as you can about the subject, and make the best decision possible.

Light for Viewing

Even if you don't think that full-spectrum lighting is necessary for your lizard's health, you may want to use some form of lighting to help make your gecko and his habitat easier to view.

But you must realize that, as a nocturnal lizard, your gecko probably won't come out very often while the lights are on. Nevertheless, there is nothing wrong with providing some low-level lighting for your lizard's habitat.

If you use a heat lamp to provide a thermal gradient, the light from the bulb will provide more than enough illumination to appreciate your pet's habits and habitat.

But you can also add a fluorescent fixture to your pet's cage to illuminate it. An ordinary fluorescent bulb will suffice for this purpose, but you can also select a premium model, designed to produce more balanced light. This will make the colors in the cage more appealing, and it may help your plants to stay healthier.

You can also use a red-colored light at night. This will allow you to observe your lizard as he hunts and forages during his active period, but it won't disturb him, either.

In all cases, it is important to ensure that these additional lights do not raise the cage temperature above your target zone.

Light for Health

As stated earlier, most keepers believe that full-spectrum lighting is unnecessary for tokay gecko maintenance. In fact, it probably carries some risks. Strong UV rays may be able to harm the skin of sensitive reptiles, and it may alter vitamin D metabolism in undesired ways.

In practice, tokay geckos will likely hide from the light – in fact, all reptiles housed in cages with UV-producing lights should be offered shade from the lights in at least some portion of the cage. Many reptiles are capable of seeing UV rays, and some "dose" themselves with optimal amounts of exposure. Nocturnal lizards probably don't require UV lighting, and most avoid bright conditions as a matter of practice.

Tokay geckos are frequently seen near outdoor lights.

However, those keepers who desire to include full-spectrum lighting as a component of their gecko's care, or who want to understand the reasons *some* lizards require full-spectrum lighting, must first understand a little bit about light.

Light is a type of energy that physicists call electromagnetic radiation; it travels in waves. These waves may differ in amplitude, which correlates to the vertical distance between consecutive wave crests and troughs, frequency, which correlates with the number of crests per unit of time, and wavelength.

Wavelength is the distance from one crest to the next, or one trough to the next. Wavelength and frequency are inversely proportional, meaning that as the wavelength increases, the frequency decreases. It is more common for reptile keepers to discuss wavelengths rather than frequencies.

The sun produces energy (light) with a very wide range of constituent wavelengths. Some of these wavelengths fall within a range called the visible spectrum; humans can detect these rays with their eyes. Such waves have wavelengths between about 390 and 700 nanometers. Rays with wavelengths longer or shorter than these limits are broken into their own groups and given different names.

Those rays with around 390 nanometer wavelengths or less are called ultraviolet rays or UV rays. UV rays are broken down into three different categories, just as the different colors correspond with different wavelengths of visible light. UVA rays have wavelengths between 315 to 400 nanometers, while UVB rays have wavelengths between 280 and 315 nanometers while UVC rays have wavelengths between 100 and 280 nanometers.

Rays with wavelengths of less than 280 nanometers are called x-rays and gamma rays. At the other end of the spectrum, infrared rays have wavelengths longer than 700 nanometers; microwaves and radio waves are even longer.

UVA rays are important for food recognition, appetite, activity and eliciting natural behaviors in some species. UVB rays are necessary for many reptiles to produce vitamin D3. Without this vitamin, sun-dependent reptiles cannot properly metabolize their calcium.

Chapter 9: Substrate and Furniture

Once you have purchased or constructed your gecko's enclosure, you must place appropriate items inside it. In general, these items take the form of an appropriate substrate and the proper cage furniture, which may include live plants, hiding locations and perches for climbing.

Substrate

Substrate is a contentious issue among gecko keepers. Some keepers prefer to use a substrate, while others prefer to keep the cage floor bare. Both approaches have their merits.

Bare Enclosure Floors (No Substrate)

If you are using an enclosure with a plastic, glass or laminated floor, you can avoid using any substrate at all. The primary benefit to this approach is that you do not have to worry about your pet inadvertently ingesting some of the substrate during feeding activities.

By skipping the substrate, you can also avoid having to replace it periodically as well as the small associated expense. However, substrate-free maintenance requires more maintenance, as the cage bottom must be cleaned daily.

One drawback to substrate-free husbandry is that water will begin to pool on the cage floor if you mist the cage. This can be messy and accelerate the growth of bacterial colonies.

Substrate-free maintenance is best suited for maintaining hatchlings and juveniles, particularly when they are housed in groups. This approach allows the keeper to reduce the chances that the hatchlings will ingest substrate.

Cypress Mulch

Cypress mulch is a popular substrate choice for tokay geckos. It not only looks attractive and holds humidity well, but cypress mulch typically has a pleasant odor.

One drawback to cypress mulch is that some brands (or individual bags among otherwise good brands) produce a stick-like mulch, rather than mulch composed of thicker pieces. These sharp sticks can injure the keeper and the kept. It usually only takes one cypress mulch splinter jammed under a keeper's fingernail to cause them to switch substrates.

Cypress mulch does represent an ingestion hazard, so keepers using it should always be alert for signs that a captive has consumed anything other than food. Additionally, the numerous nooks and crannies produced by the mulch will provide insects with places to hide.

Cypress mulch is available from most home improvement and garden centers, as well as pet supply retailers. No matter the source you use, be sure that the product contains 100 percent cypress mulch without any demolition or salvage content.

Fir (Orchid) Bark
The bark of fir trees is often used for orchid propagation, and so it is often called "orchid bark." Orchid bark is very attractive, and, thanks to its relatively uniform shape, does not represent as much of an ingestion hazard as cypress mulch does. However, it is still wise to use a feeding cup if you elect to cover the bottom of the cage with this substrate.

Orchid bark absorbs water very well, so it is useful for species that require high humidity, such as tokay geckos. Additionally, orchid bark is easy to spot clean. However, monthly replacement can be expensive for those living in the Eastern United States and Europe.

Soils
Soil is another acceptable substrate for tokay geckos. You can make a suitable soil substrate by digging up your own soil, purchasing organic soil products or mixing your own blend.

Avoid products containing perlite, manure, fertilizers, pre-emergent herbicides or other additives. Sterilization of the soil before adding it to the enclosure is not strictly necessary; in fact, many of the microorganisms present will help breakdown waste products from your lizard.

Paper Products

Newspaper, paper towels and commercial cage liners are acceptable for use with tokay geckos, but they offer few benefits over a bare floor. The only real benefit paper substrates offer gecko keepers is that they make it easier to clean the cage floor – you can simply remove the paper each day and replace it with a fresh sheet.

However, paper substrates give insects places to hide, so be sure to check underneath the paper periodically, and flush out any hiding insects.

Substrate Comparison Chart

Substrate	Pros	Cons
No Substrate	No ingestion hazard. Easy to spot clean and sterilize. Free.	Unattractive. Water pools on surface.
Soil	Absorbs and retains water and easy to spot clean.	Ingestion hazard. Messy.
Cypress Mulch	Absorbs and retains water, attractive and easy to spot clean.	Ingestion hazard. Messy. Provides hiding places for insects.
Fir (Orchid) Bark	Absorbs and retains water, attractive and easy to spot clean.	Ingestion hazard. Messy. Expensive.
Newspaper	Absorbs *some* water. Safe, low-cost. Easy to maintain.	Unattractive. Provides hiding places for insects.
Commercial Paper Products	Absorbs *some* water. Safe, low-cost. Easy to maintain and keep clean.	Provides hiding places for insects. Can be expensive.

Substrates to Avoid

Some substrates are completely inappropriate for gecko maintenance, and should be avoided at all costs. These include:

- Aspen or Pine Shavings – Wood shavings (as opposed to shredded bark or mulch) are not appropriate substrates for tokay geckos. In addition to representing a choking hazard, wood shavings will quickly rot if they become wet.

- **Cedar Shavings** – Cedar shavings produce toxic fumes that may sicken or kill your gecko. Always avoid cedar shavings.

- **Sand** – Sand is too dusty for tokay geckos. It will also stick to feeder insects and find its way into your lizard's digestive tract.

- **Gravel** – You can use large gravel as a substrate, but its problems outweigh its benefits. Gravel must be washed when soiled, which is laborious and time consuming. Gravel is also quite heavy, which can cause headaches for the keeper.

- **Artificial Turf** – Although it seems like a viable option with a number of benefits, artificial turf is not a good substrate for geckos. Keeping artificial turf clean is difficult, and the threads may come loose and wrap around your lizard's tail, tongue or toes.

Cage Furniture

To complete your tokay gecko's habitat, you must provide him with visual barriers to help keep his stress level low, and perches, which he can use to travel through his cage.

A great way to provide visual barriers for your tokay geckos is to add cork slabs, cardboard tubes, sections of egg crate or live plants to the enclosure.

All perches must be safe, easy to clean and securely attached to the enclosure. Most keepers opt for real branches, but you can also use commercially produced plastic vines or branches.

Cork bark

The outer bark of the cork oak (*Quercus suber*), cork bark is available in both tubes and flat slabs. Either work well for tokay gecko maintenance, although flat slabs can be arranged to provide your lizard with snugger hiding places.

The primary downsides to cork bark relate to its price (it is often rather expensive) and its tendency to collect debris in the cracks on its surface, which makes cleaning difficult.

Cardboard and Other Disposable Hides

Cardboard tubes, boxes or sheets also make excellent hiding spaces, as do sections of foam egg crate. These materials are light weight, very low cost and easy to replace once soiled.

Try to arrange these items in ways that mimic the hiding places tokay geckos would use in the wild. For example, tokay geckos like to hide under tree bark, so place a stack of cardboard sheets or tubes in a clump on one side of the habitat.

Plants

Live plants may require more work and effort on the part of the keeper, but they offer several benefits for your pet. In addition to providing a place for your pet to slip out of sight, live plants increase the humidity of the enclosure. Some plants can also provide enough perching opportunities that you needn't use any additional perches in the enclosure.

Always wash all plants before placing them in the enclosure to help remove any pesticide residues. It is also wise to discard the potting soil used for the plant and replace it with fresh soil, which you know contains no pesticides, perlite or fertilizer.

While you can plant cage plants directly in soil substrates, this complicates maintenance and makes it difficult to replace the substrate regularly. Accordingly, it is generally preferable to keep the plant in some type of container. Be sure to use a catch tray under the pot, so that water draining from the container does not flow into the cage.

You must use care to select a species that will thrive in your gecko's enclosure. For example, species that require direct sunlight will perish in the relatively dim light in your pet's home.

Instead, you must choose plants that will thrive in shaded conditions. Similarly, because you will be misting the cage regularly, and trying to keep the internal environment as humid as possible, few succulents or other plants adapted to arid habitats will live in a tokay gecko enclosure.

You must also consider the growth habit and characteristics of the plants you intend to use. For example, ground covers will not prove of much use to arboreal lizards. You need plants that not only grow vertically, but you need plants that provide comfortable perching opportunities for the lizards. The plants should also have broad leaves, which will allow them to serve as visual barriers and also provide a good surface from which your tokay gecko will drink water.

Perches

You can purchase climbing branches from pet and craft stores, or you can collect them yourself. When collecting your own branches, try to use branches that are still attached to trees (always obtain permission first). Such branches will harbor fewer insects and other invertebrate pests than dead branches will.

Many different types of branches can be used in tokay gecko cages. Most non-aromatic hardwoods suffice. See the chart below for specific recommendations.

Whenever collecting wood to be used as perches, bring a ruler so that you can visualize how large the branch will be, once it is back in the cage. Leave several inches of spare material at each end of the branch; this way, you can cut the perch to the correct length, once you arrive back home.

Always wash branches with plenty of hot water and a stiff, metal-bristled scrub brush to remove as much dirt, dust and fungus as possible before placing them in your pet's cage. Clean stubborn spots with a little bit of dish soap, but be sure to rinse them thoroughly afterwards.

It is also advisable to sterilize branches before placing them in a cage. The easiest way to do so is by placing the branch in a 300-degree oven for about 15 minutes. Doing so should kill the vast majority of pests and pathogens lurking inside the wood.

Some keepers like to cover their branches with a water-sealing product. This is acceptable if a non-toxic product is used and the branches are allowed to air dry for several days before being placed in the cage. However, as branches are relatively easy to replace, it is not necessary to seal them if you plan to replace them.

When placing the perches in the cage, be sure to do so in a way that allows your pet to access all areas of the cage. Try to strike a good balance between offering your pet plenty of perches, without overly crowding the habitat.

You can often place branches diagonally across the enclosure, in such a way that alleviates the need for direct attachment to the cage. However, horizontal branches will require secure points of attachment so they do not fall and injure your pet.

You can attach the branches to the cage in a variety of different ways. Be sure to make it easy to remove the branches as necessary, so you can clean them or transfer your lizard without having to handle him.

You can use hooks and eye-screws to suspend branches, which allows for quick and easy removal, but it is only applicable for cages with walls that will accept and support the eye-screws. You can also make "closet rod holders" by cutting a slot into small PVC caps, which are attached to the cage frame.

Recommended Species

Maple trees (*Acer* spp.)

Oak trees (*Quercus* spp.)

Walnut trees (*Juglans* spp.)

Ash trees (*Fraxinus* spp.)

Dogwood trees (*Cornus* spp.)

Sweetgum trees (*Liquidambar stryaciflua*)

Crepe Myrtle trees (*Lagerstroemia* spp.)

Willow trees (*Salix* spp.)

Tuliptrees (*Liriodendron tulipifera*)

Pear trees (*Pyrus* spp.)

Apple trees (*Malus* spp.)

Manzanitas (*Arctostaphylos* spp.)

Grapevine (*Vitis* spp.)

Species To Avoid

Cherry trees (*Prunus* spp.)

Pine trees (*Pinus* spp.)

Cedar trees (*Cedrus* spp., etc.)

Juniper trees (*Juniperus* spp.)

Poison ivy / oak (*Toxicodendron* spp.)

Chapter 10: Maintaining the Captive Habitat

Now that you have acquired your lizard and set up the enclosure, you must develop a protocol for maintaining his habitat. While gecko habitats require major maintenance every month or so, they only require minor daily maintenance.

In addition to designing a husbandry protocol, you must embrace a record-keeping system to track your lizard's growth and health.

Cleaning and Maintenance Procedures

Once you have decided on the proper enclosure for your pet, you must keep your lizard fed, hydrated and ensure that the habitat stays in proper working order to keep your captive healthy and comfortable.

Some tasks must be completed each day, while others are should be performed weekly, monthly or annually.

Daily

- Monitor the ambient and surface temperatures of the habitat.

- Provide drinking water by misting the cage.

- Spot clean the cage to remove any loose insects, feces, urates or pieces of shed skin.

- Ensure that the lights, latches and other moving parts are in working order.

- Verify that your lizard is acting normally and appears healthy. You do not necessarily need to handle him to do so.

- Feed your lizard a few insects (some keepers only feed their captives three or four times per week).

- Ensure that the humidity and ventilation are at appropriate levels.

Weekly

- Change sheet-like substrates (newspaper, paper towels, etc.).

- Clean the inside surfaces of the enclosure.

- Inspect your lizard closely for any signs of injury, parasites or illness.

- Wash and sterilize all food dishes.

Monthly
- Break down the cage completely, remove and discard particulate substrates.

- Sterilize drip containers and similar equipment in a mild bleach solution.

- Measure and weigh your lizard.

- Photograph your pet (recommended, but not imperative).

- Prune any plants as necessary.

Annually
- Replace the batteries in your thermometers and any other devices that use them.

Cleaning your lizard's cage and furniture is relatively simple. Regardless of the way it became soiled, the basic process remains the same:

1. Rinse the object
2. Using a scrub brush or sponge and soapy water, remove any organic debris from the object.
3. Rinse the object thoroughly.
4. Disinfect the object.
5. Re-rinse the object.
6. Dry the object.

Chemicals & Tools
A variety of chemicals and tools are necessary for reptile care. Save yourself some time by purchasing dedicated cleaning products and keeping them in the same place that you keep your tools.

Spray Bottles
Misting your gecko and his habitat with fresh water is one of the best ways to provide him with water. You can do this with a small,

handheld misting bottle or a larger, pressurized unit (such as those used to spray herbicides). Automated units are available, but they are rarely cost-effective unless you are caring for a large colony of tokay geckos.

Scrub Brushes or Sponges
It helps to have a few different types of scrub brushes and sponges on hand for scrubbing and cleaning different items. Use the least abrasive sponge or brush suitable for the task to prevent wearing out cage items prematurely. Do not use abrasive materials on glass or acrylic surfaces. Steel-bristled brushes work well for scrubbing coarse, wooden items, such as branches.

Spatulas and Putty Knives
Spatulas, putty knives and similar tools are often helpful for cleaning reptile cages. For example, urates (which are not soluble in anything short of hot lava) often become stuck on cage walls or furniture. Instead of trying to dissolve them with harsh chemicals, just scrape them away with a sturdy plastic putty knife.

Spatulas and putty knives can also be helpful for removing wet newspaper, which often becomes stuck to the floor of the cage.

Small Vacuums
Small, handheld vacuums are very helpful for sucking up the dust left behind from substrates. They are also helpful for cleaning the cracks and crevices around the cage doors. A shop vacuum, with suitable hoses and attachments, can also be helpful, if you have enough room to store it.

Steam Cleaners
Steam cleaners are very effective for sterilizing cages, water bowls and durable cage props after they have been cleaned. In fact, steam is often a better choice than chemical disinfectants, as it will not leave behind a toxic residue. Never use a steam cleaner near your lizard, the plants in his cage or any other living organisms.

Soap
Use a gentle, non-scented dish soap. Antibacterial soap is preferred, but not necessary. Most people use far more soap than is necessary -- a few drops mixed with a quantity of water is usually sufficient to help remove surface pollutants.

Bleach

Bleach (diluted to one-half cup per gallon of water) makes an excellent disinfectant. Be careful not to spill any on clothing, carpets or furniture, as it is likely to discolor the objects.

Always be sure to rinse objects thoroughly after using bleach and be sure that you cannot detect any residual odor. Bleach does not work as a disinfectant when in contact with organic substances; accordingly, items must be cleaned before you can disinfect them.

Veterinarian Approved Disinfectant

Many commercial products are available that are designed to be safe for their pets. Consult with your veterinarian about the best product for your situation, its method of use and its proper dilution.

Avoid Phenols

Always avoid cleaners that contain phenols, as they are extremely toxic to some reptiles. In general, do not use household cleaning products to avoid exposing your pet to toxic chemicals.

Keeping Records

It is important to keep records regarding your pet's health, growth and feeding, as well as any other important details. In the past, reptile keepers would do so on small index cards or in a notebook. In the modern world, technological solutions may be easier. For example, you can use your computer or mobile device to keep track of the pertinent info about your pet.

You can record as much information about your pet as you like, and the more information to you record, the better. But minimally, you should record the following:

Pedigree and Origin Information

Be sure to record the source of your lizard, the date on which you acquired him and any other data that is available. Breeders will often provide customers with information regarding the sire, dam, date of birth, weights and feeding records, but other sources will rarely offer comparable data.

Feeding Information

Record the date of each feeding, as well as the type of food item(s) offered. It is also helpful to record any preferences you may observe or any meals that are refused.

It is also wise to record the times you supplement the food with calcium or vitamin powders, unless you employ a standard weekly protocol.

Weights and Length

Because you look at your pet frequently, it is difficult to appreciate how quickly he is (or isn't) growing. Accordingly, it is important to track his size diligently.

Weigh your gecko with a high quality digital scale. The scale must be sensitive to one-tenth-gram increments to be useful for very small lizards.

It is often easiest to use a dedicated "weighing container" with a known weight to measure your gecko. This way, you will not have to keep the lizard stationary on the scale's platform – you can simply place him in the container and place the entire container on the scale. Subtract the weight of the container to obtain the weight of your lizard.

If you are able to incorporate removable perches in the cage, record the weight of the perch so that you can simply manipulate the gecko's perch rather than having to pry your lizard from his perch. Just weigh the lizard on his perch, subtract the weight of the perch and record the difference as the lizard's weight.

You can measure your lizard's length as well, but it is not as important as tracking his weight. Be sure to measure his snout-vent length, rather than his total length, in case he eventually loses his tail.

One easy way to get an approximation of your gecko's length is to place him in a clear-bottomed container, alongside a ruler. Lift the container above your head and look through the bottom of the container to compare your lizard's length against the ruler.

Maintenance Information

Record all of the noteworthy events associated with your pet's care. While it is not necessary to note that you misted the cage each day, it is appropriate to record the dates on which you changed the substrate or sterilized the cage.

Whenever you purchase new equipment, supplies or caging, note the date and source. This not only helps to remind you when you purchased the items, but it may help you track down a source for the items in the future, if necessary.

Breeding Information

If you intend to breed your lizard, you should record all details associated with pre-breeding conditioning, cycling, introductions, matings, color changes, copulations and egg deposition.

Record all pertinent information about any resulting clutches as well, including the number of viable eggs, as well as the number of unhatched and unfertilized eggs (often called "slugs" by reptile keepers).

Additionally, if you keep several lizards together in the same enclosure, you'll want to be careful to document the details of egg deposition, so you can be sure you know the correct parentage of each egg.

Record Keeping Samples

The following are two different examples of suitable recording systems.

The first example is reminiscent of the style employed by many with large collections. Because such keepers often have numerous animals, the notes are very simple, and require a minimum amount of writing or typing.

The second example demonstrates a simple approach that is employed by many with small collections (or a single pet): keeping notes on paper. Such notes could be taken in a notebook or journal, or you could type directly into a word processor. It does not matter *how* you keep records, just that you *do* keep records.

ID Number: 44522		Genus: Species/Sub:	Gekko gecko	Gender: DOB:	Male 3/20/15	CARD #2
6.30.15 Crickets	7.03.15 Super Worms	7.08.15 Super Worms	7.14.15 Crickets	7.17.15 Roaches		
7.01.15 Crickets	7.05.15 Crickets	7.09.15 Roaches	7.15.15 Roaches	7.19.15 Sterilized Cage		
7.02.15 Roaches	7.06.15 Crickets	7.12.15 Crickets	7.16.15 Crickets			

Date	Notes
4-22-13	*Acquired "Cujo" the tokay gecko from a lizard breeder named Mark at the in-town reptile expo. Mark explained that Cujo's scientific name is Gekko gecko. Cost was $30. Mark said he purchased the lizard in March, but he does not know the exact date.*
4-23-13	*Cujo spent the night in the container I bought him in. I purchased a small plastic storage box cage, a heat lamp and a thermometer at the hardware store, and I ordered a non-contact thermometer online. I found and cleaned a few branches from outside, and a pothos plant so he had places to climb and hide*
4-27-13	*Cujo eagerly drank when I misted him. He was also hungry! He ate 12 crickets in about 5 minutes.*
4-29-13	*I fed Cujo 12 crickets today. He ate them as quickly as the first feeding*
5-1-13	*Since Cujo looked hungry, I fed him a few roaches today. I caught them outside, but I'll start buying some too.*
5-3-13	*Fed Cujo a dozen crickets and a moth that flew into the house. He ate everything and looked like he wanted more.*

Chapter 11: Feeding Tokay Geckos

Like most other geckos, tokay geckos feed on invertebrates. However, they also include a variety of small vertebrates in their diet when the opportunity arises.

The best captive diet for tokay geckos is one that mimics their wild diet, being comprised of a diverse mix of gut-loaded insects. You can provide them with the occasional pinky mouse, but this is not necessary. By gut-loading your insects (feeding them nutritious fruits and vegetables before feeding the insects to your gecko) and using a diverse array of insects, you can help reduce the chances that your gecko's diet will be deficient in some area.

Nevertheless, providing a varied diet is not always sufficient to avoid deficiencies, so it is also wise to supplement some of your pet's food with vitamins and minerals.

Insects
Insects are a great food source for tokay geckos, whether you choose to offer them as a dietary staple or merely an occasional treat. Crickets and roaches are the best commercially produced insects to offer, but silkworms and super worms can also make up a significant portion of their total diet.

Some keepers supplement their captive's diet with wild caught insects, but discretion is advised, as such insects may be contaminated with pesticides or infested with parasites.

Prey Size
It is important to offer the right size insect prey, to prevent your pet from suffering injuries. As a rule of thumb, try to provide your lizard with insects that are no longer than the distance between your pet's eyes. This is especially important for small tokay geckos, whose eyes are frequently larger than their stomach.

Feeding Quantity and Frequency
The proper feeding frequency for a gecko depends on its size, species and age. Generally speaking, most tokay geckos should be fed four to seven times per week; the younger and smaller the lizard,

the more often it should be fed. Assuming that the lizard has access to suitable temperatures and you implement an effective supplementation regimen, you aren't likely to overfeed a young tokay gecko. However, mature lizards may become overweight if fed too frequently.

Ultimately, you must adjust your lizard's diet by monitoring his weight and tail condition. Young lizards should exhibit steady, moderate growth rates, while mature animals should maintain a relatively consistent body weight throughout the year (the body weights of mature females will obviously fluctuate over the course of a breeding season, as eggs are produced and deposited).

If your lizard begins losing weight or his tail begins shrinking, you must increase the frequency of his feedings. Conversely, those that gain excessive wait should be fed slightly less food. Just be sure to consult with your veterinarian before altering your feeding schedule drastically.

A tokay gecko in the wild.

Do not allow large numbers of feeder insects to roam the enclosure freely, as it can stress your gecko. Additionally, the crickets may feed on the delicate skin near your lizard's eyes and vent. Only give your pet as many insects as he can eat in one sitting. Once he is full, the cage should be free of insects.

Vitamin and Mineral Supplements

Many keepers add commercially produced vitamin and mineral supplements to their gecko's food on a regular basis. In theory, these supplements help to correct dietary deficiencies and ensure that captive lizards get a balanced diet. In practice, things are not this simple.

While some vitamins and minerals are unlikely to build up to toxic levels, others may very well cause problems if provided in excess. This means that you cannot simply apply supplements to every meal – you must decide upon a sensible supplementation schedule.

Additionally, it can be difficult to ascertain exactly how much of the various vitamins and minerals you will be providing to your lizard, as most such products are sold as fine powders, designed to be sprinkled on feeder insects.

This is hardly a precise way to provide the proper dose to your lizard, and the potential for grossly over- or under-estimating the amount of supplement delivered is very real.

Because the age, sex and health of your gecko all influence the amount of vitamins and minerals your pet requires, and each individual product has a unique composition, it is wise to consult your veterinarian before deciding upon a supplementation schedule. However, most keepers provide vitamin supplementation once each week, and calcium supplementation several times per week.

Chapter 12: Providing Water to Your Tokay Gecko

Like most other animals, tokay geckos require drinking water to remain healthy. However, the relative humidity (the amount of water in the air) is also an important factor in their health.

While drinking water helps to keep the lizards hydrated, the moisture in the air helps to keep their skin healthy and prevents respiratory problems from developing.

Providing Drinking Water

Providing ample drinking water is imperative to the health of your tokay gecko. While some tokay geckos will drink water from a dish, most prefer to drink droplets of water.

Accordingly, most keepers provide water to their gecko by misting the cage, the perches and plants inside the enclosure. The resulting water droplets will usually entice your gecko to lap them up greedily.

Misting provides the additional benefit of raising the cage humidity, and it tends to wash some surface pollutants from the perches and leaves.

You can mist the cage with a hand-held misting bottle, a pressurized unit or an automated misting system. An inexpensive hand-held misting bottle usually suffices for those caring for a single gecko, while those maintaining several individuals often find the latter two options more efficient.

Water Quality

Some keepers prefer to give their gecko dechlorinated or purified or spring water, but others simply offer tap water. Purified bottled water and spring water are typically safe for lizards, but distilled water should be avoided to prevent causing electrolyte imbalances.

It is wise to have tap water tested to ensure that heavy metals or other pollutants are not present before offering it to your gecko.

Humidity

Tokay geckos hail from high-humidity habitats, and it is wise to provide them with such in captive settings. In addition to helping them shed their skin more effectively, appropriate humidity is also important for the health of their respiratory system.

Tokay geckos prefer a relative humidity in the 60 to 80 percent range, although they can probably tolerate higher humidity levels, provided the habitat remains clean and well-ventilated.

Reptile keepers usually achieve such humidity levels by restricting the airflow into the cage, adding more water to the enclosure or some combination of both strategies.

Misting adds water to the cage, and because it spreads the water into tiny droplets, misting raises the humidity more quickly than simply pouring water in the cage does. However, you can also add water to the substrate or incorporate a large water dish in the enclosure to raise the humidity level.

Whichever method you choose to raise the enclosure humidity, be sure to monitor the humidity levels with a quality hygrometer, rather than simply guessing at the humidity level.

Chapter 13: Interacting with Your Tokay Gecko

Although tokay geckos will never be confused with leopard geckos, bearded dragons or other "lap lizards," some can learn to tolerate interaction with their keeper, although this will often take considerable work. Additionally, captive bred individuals are far more likely to become reasonably tame than wild caught individuals are.

Handling a Tokay Gecko

The very best way to handle your gecko is to allow him to walk on your outstretched hands and forearms, rather than physically restraining him. However, you may need to grip him gently but tightly, if you need to examine him closely.

If the lizard tries to run away or gapes its mouth threateningly when you place your hand near him, stop and try again some other time. You may need to help convince your lizard that you are not a threat by hand-feeding him for some time (just be careful!). After doing this for a while, you can try letting him crawl onto your hand again.

To pick up your tokay gecko, try to slide a finger (or two, if the individual is large) underneath the lizard's chin. Gently apply upward pressure, and the lizard will usually begin moving up your hand or finger. Keep lifting up gently and the lizard will likely crawl right onto you as though you were a tree.

You can allow your gecko to walk around on your hand for 5 or 10 minutes, provided that the lizard does not begin showing signs of stress. You can just let him walk around on your hand while you tend to minor duties in the cage, but if you must perform substantial maintenance to the habitat, it is wiser to place him in a temporary holding cage while you carry out the necessary tasks. When it is time to put him back in his enclosure, move him close to a perch or the cage wall, and allow him to crawl onto the perch on his own.

Always be patient when transferring a gecko to or from your hands. Try to "encourage" rather than "force" movements. Sometimes, tickling your gecko's foot or tail lightly will stimulate them to move more quickly.

Obviously, great care must be taken with regard to the animal's tail, which may break off at the slightest disturbance. In general, you should avoid contact with the tail as much as is possible.

In the Event of a Bite

In the event that your lizard bites, try to remain calm. Although the lizard will undoubtedly give you a strong pinch and his sharp teeth may break the skin, most bites are unlikely to cause much serious damage.

Move your hand back into the lizard's cage, and allow him to grip a perch with his feet. This will usually cause him to release the bite and dart off into the cage. If that doesn't work, you can try placing your hand under some cool, running water, which will normally cause him to let go.

Wash all bites with soap and warm water, and consult your doctor if the bite breaks the skin.

Transporting Your Pet

Although you should strive to avoid any unnecessary travel with your geckos, circumstances often demand that you do (such as when your lizard becomes ill).

Strive to make the journey as stress-free as possible for your pet. This means protecting him from physical harm, as well as blocking as much stressful stimuli as possible.

The best type of container to use when transporting your gecko is a plastic storage box. Add several ventilation holes to plastic containers to provide suitable ventilation.

Add a few paper towel tubes to the container so your gecko can hide and feel secure while traveling. Place a few paper towels or some clean newspaper in the bottom of the box to absorb any fluids, should your lizard defecate or discharge urates.

Monitor your lizard regularly, but avoid constantly opening the container to take a peak. Checking up on your pet once every half-hour or so is more than sufficient.

Pay special attention to the enclosure temperatures while traveling. Use your digital thermometer to monitor the air temperatures inside the transportation container. Try to keep the temperatures in the high-70s Fahrenheit (25 to 26 degrees Celsius) so that your pet will remain comfortable. Use the air-conditioning or heater in your vehicle as needed to keep the animal within this range.

Keep your gecko's transportation container as stable as possible while traveling. Do not jostle your pet unnecessarily and always use a gentle touch when moving the container. Never leave the container unattended.

Because you cannot control the thermal environment, it is not wise to take your lizard with you on public transportation.

Hygiene
Reptiles can carry *Salmonella* spp., *Escherichia coli* and several other zoonotic pathogens. Accordingly, it is imperative that you use good hygiene practices when handling reptiles.

Always wash your hands with soap and warm water each time you touch your pet, his habitat or the tools you use to care for him. Antibacterial soaps are preferred, but standard hand soap will suffice.

In addition to keeping your hands clean, you must also take steps to ensure your environment does not become contaminated with pathogens. In general, this means keeping your lizard and any of the tools and equipment you use to maintain his habitat separated from your belongings.

Establish a safe place for preparing his food, storing equipment and cleaning his habitat. Make sure these places are far from the places in which you prepare your food and personal effects. Never wash cages or tools in kitchens or bathrooms that are used by humans.

Always clean and sterilize any items that become contaminated by the germs from your lizard or his habitat.

Chapter 14: Common Health Concerns

Your gecko cannot tell you when he is sick; like most other reptiles, tokay geckos endure illness stoically. This does not mean that injuries and illnesses do not cause them distress, but without expressive facial features, they do not *look* like they are suffering.

In fact, reptiles typically do not display symptoms until the disease has already reached an advanced state. Accordingly, it is important to treat injuries and illnesses promptly – often with the help of a qualified veterinarian –in order to provide your pet with the best chance of recovery.

Finding a Suitable Veterinarian

Gecko keepers often find that it is more difficult to find a veterinarian to treat their lizard than it is to find a vet to treat a cat or dog. Relatively few veterinarians treat reptiles, so it is important to find a reptile-oriented vet *before* you need one. There are a number of ways to do this:

- You can search veterinarian databases to find one that is local and treats reptiles.

- You can inquire with your dog or cat vet to see if he or she knows a qualified reptile-oriented veterinarian to whom he or she can refer you.

- You can contact a local reptile-enthusiast group or club. Most such organizations will be familiar with the local veterinarians.

- You can inquire with local nature preserves or zoos. Most will have relationships with veterinarians that treat reptiles and other exotic animals.

Those living in major metropolitan areas may find a vet reasonably close, but rural reptile keepers may have to travel considerable distances to find veterinary assistance.

If you do not have a reptile-oriented veterinarian within driving distance, you can try to find a conventional veterinarian who is willing to consult with a reptile-oriented veterinarian via the phone or internet. These types of "two-for-one" visits may be expensive, as you will have to pay for both the actual visit and the consultation, but they may be your only option.

Reasons to Visit the Veterinarian

While reptiles do not require vaccinations or similar routine treatments, they may require visits to treat illnesses or injuries. However, you needn't travel to the vet every time your gecko refuses a meal or experiences a bad shed. In fact, unnecessary veterinary visits may prove more harmful than helpful, so it is important to distinguish between those ailments that require care and those that are best treated at home.

When in doubt, contact your veterinarian and solicit his or her advice before packing up your lizard and hauling him in for an office visit. However, any of the following signs or symptoms can indicate serious problems, and each requires veterinary evaluation.

Visit your veterinarian when:

- Anytime your lizard wheezes, exhibits labored breathing or produces a mucus discharge from its nostrils or mouth.

- Your lizard produces soft or watery feces for longer than 48 hours.

- He suffers any significant injury. Common examples include thermal burns, friction damage to the rostral (nose) region or injured feet.

- Reproductive issues occur, such as being unable to deliver eggs. If a lizard appears nervous, agitated or otherwise stressed and unable to expel eggs, see your veterinarian immediately.

- Your lizard fails to feed for an extended period (more than three or four days and not associated with seasonal or reproductive changes).

- Your lizard displays any unusual lumps, bumps or lesions.

- Your lizard's intestines prolapse.

Ultimately, you must make all the decisions on behalf of your lizard, so weigh the pros and cons of each veterinary trip carefully and make the best decision you can for your pet. Just be sure that you always strive to act in his best interest.

Common Health Problems

The following are a few of the most common health problems that afflict tokay geckos. Their causes and the suggested course of action are also discussed.

Retained or Poor Sheds

Tokay geckos do not shed their entire skin at one time, as snakes do. Instead, they tend to shed in numerous pieces, over several hours or days. Occasionally, this can cause them to retain portions of their old skin. While this is not usually a big problem, care must be taken to ensure that the face, tail tip and toes all shed completely. If skin is retained in these places, blood flow can be restricted, eventually causing the death of the associated tissues. Sometimes this leads to the loss of toes or tail tips.

The best way to remove retained sheds is by temporarily increasing the enclosure humidity and misting your animal more frequently. In cases involving small amounts of retained skin, this may be enough to resolve the problem within a few days.

If this does not work, you may need to remove the retained skin manually. If the skin is partially free, you can try to get a grip on the loose part and gently pull the remaining skin free (do not try this if the retained skin attaches near the eyes).

If the retained skin is not peeling up around the edges, you will not be able to grip it. In such cases, use a damp paper towel to gently rub the area in question. With a little bit of water and gentle friction, you can usually dislodge the retained skin.

Always avoid forcing the skin off, as you may injure your pet. If the skin does not come off easily, return him to his cage and try again in 12 to 24 hours. Usually, repeated dampening will loosen the skin sufficiently to be removed.

If repeated treatments do not yield results, consult your veterinarian. He may feel that the retained shed is not causing a problem, and advise you to leave it attached – it should come off with the next shed. Alternatively, it if is causing a problem, the veterinarian can remove it without much risk of harming your pet.

Respiratory Infections

Like humans, lizards can suffer from respiratory infections. Geckos with respiratory infections exhibit fluid or mucus draining from their nose and/or mouth, may be lethargic and are unlikely to eat. They may also spend excessive amounts of time basking on or under the heat source, in an effort to induce a "behavioral fever."

Bacteria, or, less frequently, fungi or parasites often cause respiratory infections. In addition, cleaning products, perfumes, pet dander and other particulate matter can irritate a reptile's respiratory tract as well. Some such bacteria and most fungi are ubiquitous, and only become problematic when they overwhelm an animal's immune system. Other bacteria and most viruses are transmitted from one lizard to another.

To reduce the chances of illnesses, keep your lizard separated from other lizards, keep his enclosure exceptionally clean and be sure to provide the best husbandry possible, in terms of temperature, ventilation and humidity. Additionally, avoid stressing your pet by handling him too frequently, or exposing him to chaotic situations.

Veterinary care is almost always required to treat respiratory infections. Your vet will likely take samples of the mucus and have it analyzed to determine the causal agent. The veterinarian will then prescribe medications, if appropriate, such as antibiotics.

It is imperative to carry out the actions prescribed by your veterinarian exactly as stated, and keep your lizard's stress level very low while he is healing. Stress can reduce immune function, so avoid handling him unnecessarily, and consider covering the front of his cage while he recovers.

"Mouth Rot"

Mouth rot – properly called stomatitis – is identified by noting discoloration, discharge or cheesy-looking material in your gecko's mouth. Mouth rot can be a serious illness, and requires the attention of your veterinarian.

While mouth rot can follow an injury (such as happens when a lizard rubs his snout against the sides of the cage) it can also arise from systemic illness. Your veterinarian will cleanse your lizard's mouth and potentially prescribe an antibiotic.

Your veterinarian may recommend withholding food until the problem is remedied. Always be sure that lizards recovering from mouth rot have immaculately clean habitats, with appropriate temperature, humidity and ventilation, as well as ideal temperatures.

Internal Parasites

In the wild, most geckos carry some internal parasites. While it may not be possible to keep a reptile completely free of internal parasites, it is important to keep these levels in check.

Consider any wild-caught animals to be parasitized until proven otherwise. While most captive bred geckos should have relatively few internal parasites, they are not immune to them.

Preventing parasites from building to pathogenic levels requires strict hygiene. Many parasites build up to dangerous levels when lizards are kept in cages that are continuously contaminated from feces.

Most internal parasites that are of importance for lizards are transmitted via the fecal-oral route. This means that eggs (or a similar life stage) of the parasites are released with the feces. If the lizard inadvertently ingests these, the parasites can develop inside his body and cause increased problems.

Parasite eggs are usually microscopic and easily carried by gentle drafts, where they may stick to cage walls or land in the feeding dish. Later, when the gecko snaps up an insect, he ingests the eggs as well.

Internal parasites may cause your lizard to vomit, pass loose stools, fail to grow or refuse food entirely. Other parasites may produce no obvious symptoms at all, despite causing considerable damage to your pet's internal organs. This illustrates the importance of routine fecal examinations (which do not necessarily require that you bring your pet into the office).

Your veterinarian will usually examine your pet's feces if he suspects internal parasites. By looking at the type of eggs inside the feces, your veterinarian can prescribe an appropriate medication. Many parasites are easily treated with anti-parasitic medications, but often, these medications must be given several times to eradicate the pathogens completely.

Some parasites may be transmissible to people, so always take proper precautions, including regular hand washing and keeping reptiles and their cages away from kitchens and other areas where foods are prepared.

Examples of common internal parasites include roundworms, tapeworms and amoebas.

External Parasites
Geckos can theoretically suffer from external parasites, such as ticks and mites, but this appears to be a relatively rare occurrence.

Ticks should be removed manually. Using tweezers grasp the tick as close as possible to the lizard's skin and pull with steady, gentle pressure. Do not place anything over the tick first, such as petroleum jelly, or carry out any other "home remedies," such as burning the tick with a match. Such techniques may cause the tick to inject more saliva (which may contain diseases or bacteria) into the gecko's body.

Drop the tick in a jar of isopropyl alcohol to kill it. It is a good idea to bring these to your veterinarian for analysis. Do not contact ticks with your bare hands, as many species can transmit disease to humans.

Mites are another matter entirely. While ticks are generally large enough to see easily, mites are about the size of a pepper flake. Whereas tick infestations usually only tally a few individuals, mite infestations may include thousands of individual parasites.

Mites may afflict wild caught lizards, but, as they are not confined to a small cage, such infestations are usually self-limiting. However, in captivity, mite infestations can approach plague proportions.

After a female mite feeds on a lizard, she drops off and finds a safe place (such as a tiny crack in a cage or among the substrate) to deposit her eggs. After the eggs hatch, they travel back to your pet (or to other lizards in your collection) where they feed and perpetuate the lifecycle.

Whereas a few mites may represent little more than an inconvenience to the lizard, a significant infection stresses them considerably, and may even cause death through anemia. This is particularly true for small or young animals. Additionally, mites may transmit disease from one animal to another.

There are a number of different methods for eradicating a mite infestation. In each case, there are two primary steps that must be taken: You must eradicate the lizard's parasites as well as the parasites in the environment (which includes the room in which the cage resides).

Soaking is often an effective strategy for ridding a lizard of mites, but it is not a viable option for arboreal geckos. In most cases a chemical treatment will be necessary. Consult with your veterinarian, who can recommend a prudent treatment.

You will also need to perform a thorough cage cleaning to eliminate the problem. To do so, you must remove everything from the cage, including water dishes, substrates and cage props. Sterilize all impermeable cage items, and discard the substrate and all porous cage props – including plants and trees. Vacuum the area around the cage and wipe down all of the nearby surfaces with a wet cloth.

It may be necessary to repeat this process several times to eradicate the mites completely. Accordingly, the very best strategy is to avoid contracting mites in the first place. This is why it is important to purchase your gecko from a reliable breeder or retailer, and keep him quarantined from potential mite vectors.

Long-Term Anorexia
While geckos may refuse the occasional meal, they should not fast for prolonged periods of time.

The most common reasons that geckos refuse food are improper temperatures and illness. Parasites and bacterial infections can also cause lizards to refuse food. Consult your veterinarian anytime that your pet refuses food for longer than three or four days.

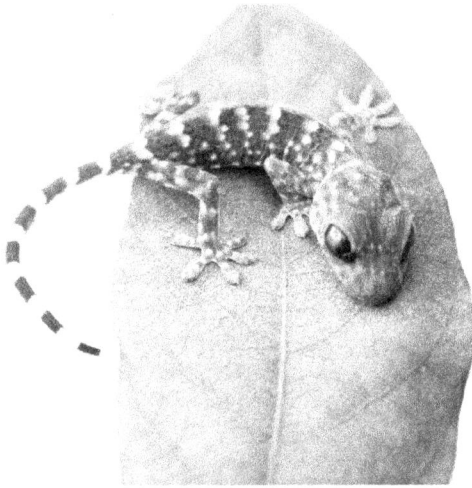

A hatchling tokay gecko.

Chapter 15: Breeding Tokay Geckos

Tokay geckos breed readily, and it is often more difficult to get them to *stop* breeding than to start leaving eggs in the cage. However, there are a few things to keep in mind to give you the best chance of success.

Sexing Tokay Geckos

Obviously, you must have at a sexual pair of animals to hope for viable eggs and eventual offspring. Fortunately, the sex of tokay geckos is relatively easy to discern. Juveniles, by contrast, are more difficult to identify as male or female.

Mature male tokay geckos can be distinguished from mature females by noting the presence of waxy secretions emerging from the pores on their inner thighs. Females have pores, but will not produce visible secretions.

You may be able to distinguish between the sexes by looking for the presence of hemipenal bulges near the lizard's tail base, but this is not as easy to do with tokay geckos as it is with some other species.

Pre-Breeding Conditioning

Breeding reptiles always entails risk, so it is wise to refrain from breeding any animals that are not in excellent health. Breeding is especially stressful for female geckos, who must withstand potential injuries during mating, and produce numerous, nutrient-rich eggs.

Animals slated for breeding trials must have excellent body weight, but obesity is to be avoided, as it is associated with reproductive problems. Ensure that the lizards are appropriately hydrated, and are free of parasites, infections and injuries.

Additionally, it is important that any females slated for breeding programs have adequate calcium stores.

Cycling

Cycling is the terms used to describe the climactic changes keepers impose upon their animals, which seek to mimic the natural seasonal changes in an animal's natural habitat.

For example, keepers may simulate a rainy season by increasing the amount of water used when misting the cage and increasing the frequency of these mistings. These changes are often helpful for stimulating captive tokay geckos into producing eggs, sperm and mating.

However, cycling is not always necessary for successful reproduction. Male and female tokay geckos usually exhibit breeding behaviors anytime the temperatures are warm and photoperiod 12-hours-long or better.

Pairing

Once your tokay geckos have reached maturity, it is time to begin introducing the male to the female. Note that tokay geckos typically work best in 1:1 ratios; they do not do well in communal or harem-style groupings.

Use care when making introductions, as males are sometimes overly aggressive when attempting to mate. Remove the male from his enclosure, and gently place him inside the female's cage.

You can leave the male with the female, but check on them periodically to ensure the pair are not antagonistic toward each other. Try not to disturb the lizards any more than necessary during the process.

Copulation may begin almost immediately, or it may take several hours to occur. The pair may copulate only once, or they may copulate several times over many days. It is usually wise to house the pair together for several days, to allow for multiple copulations, thereby helping to ensure good fertility.

After successful mating, some keepers allow the pair to continue to cohabitate, while others remove them at this time. It is probably safer to remove the male after breeding trials, but plenty of breeders keep pairs together over the long term.

With some luck, the female will become gravid (pregnant) shortly after the animals have bred. However, you may not notice that your female is gravid until she begins depositing eggs, so it is a good idea to go ahead and prepare for such an occurrence once you begin male-female introductions.

Gravid females may alter their behavior in several subtle ways. They may begin frequenting the warmer portions of the habitat, or they may become more reclusive. After initially exhibiting an increased appetite, they typically cease feeding as oviposition (egg deposition) approaches.

Egg Incubation

Over the course of the season, females may produce three or four clutches, each of which normally contains two eggs.

Tokay geckos generally deposit their eggs on the sides of the cage walls or on some other elevated perch. It is generally best to leave the eggs undisturbed, or the female may stop depositing eggs.

The eggs usually hatch in about 3 to 4 months' time.

Females appear to guard their eggs at times, and they'll usually eat the shells after the young emerge.

Neonatal Husbandry

Once the young begin hatching from their eggs, you can remove them from the parental cage and place them in a small cage or "nursery." Some keepers allow the young to remain in the adult habitat, but this exposes them to unnecessary risks.

A scaled-down version of an adult habitat, such as a small plastic storage box, makes a satisfactory nursery. Place several small perches for climbing and pieces of crumpled paper or plant clippings to provide the young with some form of cover.

Mist the young several times per day and keep the temperatures between about 80 and 86 degrees Fahrenheit (26 and 30 degrees Celsius). You can initiate feeding trials within a day or two, but most will not begin to feed until after their first shed.

Keep the young in the nursery until they begin feeding regularly. At this point, you can begin breaking them into small groups and placing them in individual enclosures.

Chapter 16: Further Reading

Never stop learning more about your new pet's natural history, biology and captive care. This is the only way to ensure that you are providing your new pet with the highest quality of life possible.

It's always more fun to watch your gecko than read about him, but by accumulating more knowledge, you'll be better able to provide him with a high quality of life.

Books

Bookstores and online book retailers offer a treasure trove of information that will advance your quest for knowledge. While books represent an additional cost involved in reptile care, you can consider it an investment in your pet's well-being. Your local library may also carry some books about tokay geckos, which you can borrow for no charge.

University libraries are a great place for finding old, obscure or academically oriented books about tokay geckos. You may not be allowed to borrow these books if you are not a student, but you can view and read them at the library.

Herpetology: An Introductory Biology of Amphibians and Reptiles
By Laurie J. Vitt, Janalee P. Caldwell
Top of Form
Bottom of Form
Academic Press, 2013

Understanding Reptile Parasites: A Basic Manual for Herpetoculturists & Veterinarians
By Roger Klingenberg D.V.M.
Advanced Vivarium Systems, 1997

Infectious Diseases and Pathology of Reptiles: Color Atlas and Text
Elliott Jacobson
CRC Press

Designer Reptiles and Amphibians
Richard D. Bartlett, Patricia Bartlett
Barron's Educational Series

Lizards: Windows to the Evolution of Diversity
By Eric R. Pianka, Laurie J. Vit
University of California Press

Magazines
Because magazines are typically published monthly or bi-monthly, they occasionally offer more up-to-date information than books do. Magazine articles are obviously not as comprehensive as books typically are, but they still have considerable value.

Reptiles Magazine
www.reptilesmagazine.com/
Covering reptiles commonly kept in captivity.

Practical Reptile Keeping
http://www.practicalreptilekeeping.co.uk/
Practical Reptile Keeping is a popular publication aimed at beginning and advanced hobbies. Topics include the care and maintenance of popular reptiles as well as information on wild reptiles.

Websites
The internet has made it much easier to find information about reptiles than it has ever been.

However, you must use discretion when deciding which websites to trust. While knowledgeable breeders, keepers and academics operate some websites, many who maintain reptile-oriented websites lack the same dedication and scientific rigor.

Anyone with a computer and internet connection can launch a website and say virtually anything they want about geckos. Accordingly, as with all other research, consider the source of the information before making any husbandry decisions.

The Reptile Report
www.thereptilereport.com/
The Reptile Report is a news-aggregating website that accumulates interesting stories and features about reptiles from around the world.

Kingsnake.com
www.kingsnake.com
After starting as a small website for gray-banded kingsnake enthusiasts, Kingsnake.com has become one of the largest reptile-oriented portals in the hobby. The site features classified advertisements, a breeder directory, message forums and other resources.

The Vivarium and Aquarium News
www.vivariumnews.com/
The online version of the former print publication, The Vivarium and Aquarium News provides in-depth coverage of different reptiles and amphibians in a captive and wild context.

Journals
Journals are the primary place professional scientists turn when they need to learn about geckos. While they may not make light reading, hobbyists stand to learn a great deal from journals.

Herpetologica
www.hljournals.org/
Published by The Herpetologists' League, Herpetologica, and its companion publication, Herpetological Monographs cover all aspects of reptile and amphibian research.

Journal of Herpetology
www.ssarherps.org/
Produced by the Society for the Study of Reptiles and Amphibians, the Journal of Herpetology is a peer-reviewed publication covering a variety of reptile-related topics.

Copeia
www.asihcopeiaonline.org/

Copeia is published by the American Society of Ichthyologists and Herpetologists. A peer-reviewed journal, Copeia covers all aspects of the biology of reptiles, amphibians and fish.

Nature
www.nature.com/
Although Nature covers all aspects of the natural world, many issues contain information that lizard enthusiasts are sure to find interesting.

Supplies
You can obtain most of what you need to maintain tokay geckos through your local pet store, big-box retailer or hardware store, but online retailers offer another option.

Just be sure that you consider the shipping costs for any purchase, to ensure you aren't "saving" yourself a few dollars on the product, yet spending several more dollars to get the product delivered.

Big Apple Pet Supply
http://www.bigappleherp.com
Big Apple Pet Supply carries most common husbandry equipment, including heating devices, water dishes and substrates.

LLLReptile
http://www.lllreptile.com
LLL Reptile carries a wide variety of husbandry tools, heating devices, lighting products and more.

Doctors Foster and Smith
http://www.drsfostersmith.com
Foster and Smith is a veterinarian-owned retailer that supplies husbandry-related items to pet keepers.

Support Organizations
Sometimes, the best way to learn about tokay geckos is to reach out to other keepers and breeders. Check out these organizations, and search for others in your geographic area.

The National Reptile & Amphibian Advisory Council

http://www.nraac.org/

The National Reptile & Amphibian Advisory Council seeks to educate the hobbyists, legislators and the public about reptile and amphibian related issues.

American Veterinary Medical Association

www.avma.org

The AVMA is a good place for Americans to turn if you are having trouble finding a suitable reptile veterinarian.

The World Veterinary Association

http://www.worldvet.org/

The World Veterinary Association is a good resource for finding suitable reptile veterinarians worldwide.

References

Abigail S. Tucker a, G. J. (2014). Evolution and developmental diversity of tooth regeneration. *Seminars in Cell & Developmental Biology*.

Anderson, S. P. (2003). The Phylogenetic Definition of Reptilia. *Systematic Biology*.

Hutchison, L. M. (1988). Light versus Heat: Thermoregulatory Behavior in a Nocturnal Lizard (Gekko gecko). *Herpetologica*.

RUSSELL, A. P. (1975). A contribution to the functional analysis of the foot of the Tokay, Gekko gecko (Reptilia: Gekkonidae). *Journal of Zoology*.

Ye-Zhong Tang, L.-Z. Z.-W. (2001). Advertisement Calls and Their Relation to Reproductive Cycles in Gekko gecko (Reptilia, Lacertilia). *Copeia*.

Published by IMB Publishing 2017